I

Promised

You

a

Love

Poem

To my husband,

Love,

1980

Be humble for you are made of earth.

Be noble for you are made of stars.

— *Serbian proverb*

CONTENTS

I

Promised

You

a

Love

Poem

EXILE

(and everything after)

Mixtape

We fell for you before we were
legal to drink, cupping you in our back
pockets on scraps of lined school paper,
True Love lives in mansions with pintos,
and six children in taffeta dresses
which somehow made us legitimate.

We waited, waited and then tripped
over our yearbook heartthrobs,
rolling down grassy hills,
scraped knees and lumberjacks
building secret forts and
mystic potions.
In my treasure chest under the tree,
I collected magazines and parchments,
rose-petaled carpets and daisy hair bouquets.
No detail was left unturned.

I was not alone. Girls loving boys since 1989,
before we could spell "dignified,"
we borrowed surnames that weren't ours and
knew love fell like a ballad,
floating toward us like fireflies do
with or without the spells.

Three decades in, some had babies and
others had rings while

the rest of us tried to change you.

We rubbed pennies in between
forefingers and thumbs,
flicking coins into faraway fountains,
poems that shan't be read
past the clock turn of midnight,
far past the bedtime for
boyhood.

Glass shoes lost in mirrored castles,
step-sisters to each other we wait
for you,
our dearest kin,
and pray we have not surpassed you.

Begin with him: unshaven, half-gorged, and overtly of the field. Place him alone and wait. Watch him as he pets the cattle, rides the sheep, tills the soil for seeds and glowworms. Let him smirk and bask in full delight of dates and figs and cacao leaves. Peer at him, as yet untouched, sleeping on the riverbank, fishing with a spear and line.

Tomorrow, he will do it again. And each day after in rhythmic response until, at last, after seven hundred nights of space, he'll pull you to his side from out his side: his first and only birth, undressed, undone, to look you in the eye and ask, "Just where have you been?"

Meditation

Each Tuesday is a worthy place to start. Breakfast cereals with wild mulberries. Violent pleasures: space, silence, solitude.

The quality of being still: a statue, an advance on the hysteria of togetherness. It begins at a glance, a stare, and proceeds into the fingers, the synapses, the plans that pencils can't erase.

Six nights later, it commences again: I clasp the air beside me, carve initials into trees with furrowed knives, and draw chalk circles on the cadmium that never answers back.

Chlorophyll

The leaves changed way before we ever could.

Headed toward the Oregon coast,
car loaded full of fruit for the drive,
radio full of lyrics we'd sung
a thousand times since we were nine,
home was behind us now.

We tried to catch the crimson,
the final flecks of leaves before
the barrenness begins.
Fleshly green to burnt magenta
swapped in the span of a day,
before I could start the engine.
The season: abnormally wet,
the color morphing ahead of time.
Cups lay over the floor of the car,
the spill of water pouring
past our throats.

I grasped your hand, parched dry.

Cocoon

It was our last stop before crossing the border —
La Casa de Mariposas.
For nine dollars you got to see them all,
everything the pamphlet promised,
fuzzy bodies wrapped in silk
spinning cobwebs into wings.
Heavenly bugs, flapping cherubs, and a
stand-by justice of the peace,
three hundred butterflies
from Amazon and Yucatan
flying through glass cages.

The cocoons hung silent
above our brows
next to twigs and dust pink chrysalis.
Nine months for metamorphosis,
six short weeks to fly.

Toward evening, an ivory dress emerged
eyes twinkling through the glass.
The Peace beside, the rings nearby,
the butterflies took flight.
The hollow nest kept hanging,
as we are asked to leave.

Thanksgiving

The day the balloons came to town
it took sixteen men to tie them down.
They turned the corner for a confetti explosion,
watching air burst into sky,
rainbow sparkles beckoning
sons in woven scarves to
reach beyond their fathers' shoulders
and gape at flying giants:
superheroes, singing stars,
floating through November sky
so large the groundsmen could not
tie them down,
tight-wrapped rope
connecting
heroes
back to earth,
too large to contain.

Even now, I do believe.

Trapeze

The prying of the fingers is the hardest.
The thumb curves naturally into one's hand,
pulling other digits inward.

This thumb for grasping, clinging,
the owning of pens, hands, throats,
must be unlearned.
Lean back.
Counteract the pirouette
until the hand is open, fingers flat,
webs stretched to capacity,
the nonstop let-go of forearms,
pupils, lips, the holding and
remolding of sinews
until the final release.

At the Foyer Door

Cedar floors lined with knots, nails,
and mud-stuffed cracks hold earth
from last night's rain, the children's puddle play.

The ewes got out at dusk,
he says past squash, tomatoes,
beets in open barrels picked for autumn harvest.

The corner screen swats both dogs and flies.
At the window, a brown beam, basil stalks,
and peppercorns in triads.

On the knob: a flannel shirt still dripping wet.
I am standing dry.

North of Belfast

Of course, there were the sheep.
Their gnawing on grass blades
late into morning's dew
skews my sense of quaint and Yeats.
Or perhaps the whisky cup, shot glass rim,
the bar tender's furrowed brow when asked,
What's good?
Broiled cod, dill-dressed potatoes
mashed like lava lumps, salty as cider vinegar.

Outside, gulls caw at orange helms,
brackish boats of early risers,
while horses for the plow, now linked to wired fence,
slam hooves to churn up cobblestone,
as pebbled grounds grind black.

The Guinness far from pale,
the ale that's sipped for strength,
and the plastic deck of cards too messy for the
game.
I sit with smoky men who've been here all along,
pounding steel tobacco pipes next to holy wells,
beehive huts and sidewalk plaques,
cemeteries of the lost —
One and one-half million left
with crosses on their doors,
some awaiting purgatory

and others for the rapture.
There's thousands here
to feed and drink,
there's questions here
beyond my seek,
am I awake or do I sleep,
butter spreading slowly
through my veins.

I Never Knew Your Name

I had forgotten you existed.
The way you warmed your hands and wrote
memos at midnight from the glow of Broadway,
snow pouring down the window like salted ice,
the way it trickles just before spring.

I tried to tame you,
comb the wiry mane of your ambition,
appease your glory with shouts of doubt.

I was certain I could be your shelter.

Walking past Grand Central Station,
I dropped my wallet and you appeared again
with your cardboard memo.
You returned it to me
asking for nothing.
Your weathered hands
touched mine back.
I forgot to look you in the eye.
.

I keep forgetting your answers.
The fragile cannot be outnumbered.

Smoke

I stumbled into Mexico
the same way I stumbled into you,
cross on a chain, rosary around the corner
of my pinky, wrapped so tightly
the veins no longer move,
and I stared you in the eye
the way children look at the starlight.

And I thought it was all
rubbish until I discovered where
rubbish burns — in the leaf mounds behind
the steeple where the elderly woman sits,
hands in her lap, rocking to and fro in her
plea for justice. She breathed in smoke and exhaled
poverty, wondering what the complication
was all about, ashes flecking into sky.

Dancer

Last night we watched dancers move to
Leonard Cohen on a velvet-draped stage
and eight of them leapt through the air
as a complete marriage,
as one single face in a
burnt linen sweater marched
limply in the center,
back and forth until it all frayed down,
and the music took its rest.

Too young to be old,
the clock kept churning as he, the centerpiece,
ticked onward though the pain.

Perhaps it was his persistence that kept
the joy going, the push to march
through the middle and
keep walking on through,
as Robert Frost advised —
his steps brought him forth
into the center of nowhere.

Without the ache, there is no dance,
the woman next to me whispered.

He was now a hollow shadow, a timeless piece.
And still he marched, left and right,

beating as the soldier
would a drum,
beseeching through the stage lights
so the others could keep dancing.
So he himself and she herself and me myself
could trust the battle cry of movement,
each step a rolling thunder.

This is how we learn to waltz.

Eve's Song

So much world in so few breaths.
The ceaseless attempt to return
home and churn soil with a spoon.

I lost a few goddesses while moving
East to West.
I saw a star burn bright and then tumble
into the mountains.
In that pink and chartreuse horizon,
I watched a snake shed its skin
and ask me for my own.

They say if you throw incense in the wind,
the fog will scatter in haste.
I stand still awaiting the secret.
I paint my cheeks with my fingertips,
the costume to beckon your arrival.
And though day's curtain falls
like a stage without a title,
the ensemble cannot cushion me to sleep.

I cannot minimize your absence.

Navel

This blizzard — the blindspot,
the *navel,* as Jung calls it. The center that pulls you
into the other half of the prologue, the unknown,
the prequel you cannot fathom
and actively cannot handle.

The unsafe, irrational, unwashed
beyond certainty and intelligent obtrusiveness
enters in the belly:
the chord from life to mother
the birth from where you came.

The realness in the resistance
to the goddess-shaped hole
in your questions,
answers too cumbersome for tidy.

Let the divine be untamed
like you are and like you were.
Let her break you out of deadlock,
for She shall not be domesticated.

Progress

Yesterday, I entered the science lab
and the professor asked the students
to script an explanation
for everything.
Students stood upon their desks,
dropping balls into buckets below,
flicking tiny orbs into vase-like flasks of moon dust.
(The moon dust was fake, of course.)
Soon the dust became so thick
the professor stopped the experiment,
for fear it would fail the system.

Meanwhile, the children frolicked,
covered in baking soda and stardust.

I have a hypotheses on love.
I could prove to you if you like.
It's the oxytocin neural saturation
that's bonded me to you,
the reason for my saturated pulse
is cortisol and coffee.

Next week, the students will pin frogs to boards
to study how life *was,*
the dissection very technical
kills the object that is studied.

Meanwhile, children open palms
to air they cannot see.
Meanwhile, your fingers wrap 'round my wrist,
your heart throbs through your thumb.

Meanwhile remains the proof.

Hebrew

I miss the poetry I cannot feel
when I forget the words in their native tongue,
the way the *adama* earth wraps around
the *adam* man,
his heart apulse with *dam* of blood
creating red *adom*.

And we've called her Eve but
her name is *chava*, the mother
of all the living, *chaya*,
the giver of the life of *chai*,
all writ in causation form,
she that births the future
and nurses the entire world.

And I seek the answers
darash darash,
but what about *bakash bakash*,
the seeking that requests the
one desired.

And we talk of beginnings
but forget the rhythms that spin
the fact to fiction.

Like nomads in the desert peering
at mirages of their kin,

we look and see the lighting
convinced that it is G-d.

Intro to Irony

The world will stun you open
twelve thousand three hundred times.
And then it will break you open
twice as much.

Both remain true.
Beauty alone allows nothing to be born,
including us.

Let the seed fall apart
in the barren soil and watch it germinate.
Throw down your satchel bags from castle walls
and see what is borne out of crisis.
Incorporate doubt.
Bring the leopards into the temple,
as Kafka advises,
as well as everything else that scares you
and be not allergic to the process.
Clap hands with the unfamiliar until
it becomes part of the ceremony.

Beat your palms upon your breast,
and let the empty intrude.
Wrestle with the lies
that tell you you are lost.

The Wild has a plan.

The explorers would have told you so long ago had you only stopped to listen.

The Wild is the plan.

Lightworker

There is laborious work to be done,
particularly if you believe in angels
and see how a village surrounds a child.
I actually can't wrap my head around it
any other way.
Simplicity exists.
Do you understand the implications of that?
Weep on the floor for all that will not remain
but do not collapse in addiction to
necessary unfulfillment.
That rabbit hole goes on for eons.
You were born with mirrors in your palms
reflecting light.
There is nothing to fix save yourself.
Uncover your eyelids
to the burning city inside you,
to the reason you were sent —
not for a cause or a mission
but to stand on a molten rock
with a sky that pours light from the past.
To raise your fingers from your liver to your heart.
To drop the lies.
Trust.

Moses

Let's start at the beginning, when I had a story.
When fire cracked open a mountain
and the holy ground was obvious.
It all seemed simple then —
the words finding their way
to my tongue faster than I could
tether the meaning in my palms.
And the festivities of lights
that shrieked off the side door
and the spices that fled into the
night faster than I could
inhale them.

Some call it magic,
but there was little the snake charmers
could foster to complete
with the glory.
Faith came quickly, as rapture always
does when it is engraved,
when love letters home
come as carvings etched in trees:
initial me plus initial you.
Let's create a legend.

OZ

Paris

And then there was Paris.
The debutant of the melancholy.
The lover always departing the next morning.
The dethroned kings and failed playwrights
and the restless who owe money to their
cousin leading a peace movement.

The Unitarians and Libertarians,
the dreamers and pessimists of hope
who long for forgetfulness of
past regrets, deliberate catastrophes,
and stunning personal regrets.

The land where collars get unrolled
and fingers unfurled,
where love is meant to be lonely
and aching and consistently
unfulfilled in the way that
leaves us longing at half-open
doors of seduction.
Pangs clenched with passion,
the dark lover always one
step beyond our gaze.

And still, for you, we yearn.

Sierras

Circling the forest, the leaves become my
labyrinth, snow-tipped cedars brushing
nearby branch tips, winter's preamble
to a late harvest moon.
By day, the path is muddled.
By night, the lantern of the darkened sky
points from thickets to open ravine.

If you examine the spring beneath the mud,
the water therein sparkles.
I pull a tin of water to my mouth and slurp,
patting the leftover upon my cheeks
in the way that naked children molt
in the moment of their baptism.

We walk along the stream collecting pine cones in our
palms, and when the birds brings forth the sun,
we let our questions fly.

From Santo Domingo

She's standing in her nightgown she's worn since
the day Love left, grabbing thistle-coated broomsticks
that sweep her away, over and over,
mop hitting linoleum tiles.

The corn is shoulder high.
Five stalks cover her backyard garden
where britches hang freely to dry.

The plantains are sweet this morning.

Beneath the outdoor water spicket,
she washes forks and shirts and sancocho plates
until they sparkle back the rust.

The rooster crows.
Se fue la luz, se fue el agua.

Blue plastic barrels move outside
in hopes to catch the rain.
We drink together on porch rocking chairs,
paint stripped pink and teal.

The coffee is so dark we cannot find it in our cups.

Halfway through her morning story,
Cecilia reveals her seven keys, a lock for every door.

She leaves for work selling socks and shorts
and second-hand shirts fine enough
for all to wear but her.

Se fue la luz. Se fue el agua.

Six mornings without running water
leave skin parched and taut.
She cannot now foresee the six more morns
until the water returns.

The neighbor kids make mango shakes
and serve them in tall white glasses.
Nearby, beggars beg for coins,
while party girls fold down yellow socks
to match their quinceañera dresses.

It is time to weep.
Cecilia looks me in the eye so bluntly
I swallow limoncillos whole.

The procession begins.
Cecilia, dressed in black,
covers her nightgown with a cloak.
She tells me of his story.
I understands every third word and
wait for something spectacular.

Following a parade of tambourines and candles,

the crowd assembles on cue.
Inside, weepers clutch the Virgin Mary,
while Jesus and the dead man lie on wooden tables.

I grabs Cecilia's hand.
Cecilia asks me why.

More mango shake makers stare at me.
Darkened hair and eyes smile
across mint green tiled walls.
They run to touch my hair.

I go home that night and do not wash.

Soon the mangos are no longer ripe.
The fruit-selling man rests on his cart,
languish in the sun.
There will be no dinner tonight.

Cecilia sweeps back and forth like clockwork
until the ants have found their place.
Cecilia, without regret,
has not removed her nightgown now
for thirty-three and one-half years.

Lombok

So this is how dawn smells:
water-washed scents of orchid blossoms
still wet with last night's dew.
The air is thick with the bliss of dirt,
lotus leaves full of gently crossed twigs.

So this is how day breaks:
yellow hazed peaks over star-scorched skies
and sand that's lavender when damp.
Cast iron pots sizzle turmeric and cumin,
spoons for papaya and cinnamon rice.

At four a.m., a prayer. At six a.m., a lark song.
Ginger-fused tea and honey-warmed jam,
incense burning pathways to the other side,
fog parting through the veil:
I saw God in the jasmine.

Middle

I've been there.
I know what it feels like
standing at a fake mahogany bureau
on a Suzhou December night,
the floors still shining
from Ayi's polish as a
cat bequeathed with an emperor's name
scoffs me from my couch.

It's the smell of gas fumes on the back of moped
and fish oil pastries that are baked yet cold,
as musty as the steps up to the expat bar,
dartboard hanging shyly next to the pool table,
where gin pours freely if you come straight
from work, which is always the plan.
But you never arrive
because the men stand fishing
in the grey smogged fields
where there is nothing to catch.
But still they linger, searching for Szechuan
that doesn't exist,
as I pass on the back of a borrowed scooter,
balancing the curb with my left foot
and clinging to the back of her coat
with my right as she always asks me
why.

We were decadent then —
forty dollar tickets to imported Vienna symphonies
just to pass the time because
time wasn't a rhetorical question.
None of it was.
Why I was there, streaming foreign singing contests
through an illegal television connection,
watching Phillip Phillips become
an Americana guitar strumming hero
as I swirled in a high rise,
turning thirty-two in a red dress no one would see.

I went to dinner with a Canadian narcissist.
We were supposed to see the Chinese acrobats.
Instead, we walked the park filled with
tuxes and white roses, none of which were ours.

I spent my evenings praying the smog would lift,
watching badly translated B-grade films,
falling asleep alone on a couch
while friends read my blog,
jealous of my exotic adventures of loneliness.

It was a postcard kind of town.
Every store filled with gelled pens and glitter
to write prophetic notes to your future
and mail them to yourself.
I wrote one home and sent it West that June.
I returned to America in July.

The postcard promised me everything,
but still I could not find you.

There is a place where streets go unnoted
and the shoes that footstep down the pavement
all look for one same thing.

It starts in the nameless places.

Shanghai

Never lose the magic: I typed it down
from the back seat of my driver's taxi
only two hours after I landed in Shanghai.
We drove through towns of abandoned buildings
grey cement showering smoke through stacks
of stacks on sky.

After an hour from nowhere,
I enlarged the font and
saved it as my screensaver.

Each night from my linoleum apartment,
I lit incense at my altar
full of polished rocks and folded napkins
that I scrawled on to remember,
sipping brandy
and *no thank you's*
when the dice fell on the table.

No and *thank you* were my alibis
when Mandarin flew freely,
when I could see beyond the neon lights
and ashtray-lined canals.

I flew back later that summer.

I met you in all the wrong ways

as British-laden drinks poured over
dim sum, chopsticks, and saki.
We fought for social justice that night,
through film, hors d'oeuvres, and cocktails.

You told me that you wrote.
I wondered about your screen saver.

A few weeks after, I picked you up
on the corner of Victoria and State.
I was running behind,
and you were running early.
It took me four changed outfits before I left
my house for dinner.

Halfway through pho and vermicelli,
I told myself that your eyes were too kind
and that you said your "S's" strange
and a few other lies to prevent my cheeks
from revealing all of my secrets.

I wasn't yet comfortable in pink.

We watched more films that night.
I talked of India and screenplays
and you said, *I'll help you with that.*
You placed your hand upon my back.
I didn't wash my shirt.

We ate breakfast at the Daily Bread
and walked the farmer's markets.
I gaped at all the begonia beds while
you grabbed back my palms.

I wanted to give you poetry,
my journals and my scrapbooks.
I read you stanzas you could not understand,
skipping lines to condense the story.
We wrapped ourselves in stars and blankets,
pretending we were royals.

The fireworks were especially bright
on the eve of January first.
We watched them atop a crowded town,
welcoming another year.
Xie xie, I said, my Mandarin full,
while the waiter handed us fortunes.

Mine read, *Never give up the magic.*

Mystics

She was carried by dragons
past lords and ladies,
hanging Asian lanterns which
were all too wrong for her.

Tell me if it's too far for you
to sit on the bank of a faraway country
in Istanbul or Reykjavik
and search for four leaf clovers.

We were promised the great life,
the feast of Franciscan kings,
the respite of hallowed walls near the monastery's
edge that would protect us from harm.

Sleeping Beauty, gentle Rose,
we owed you a fable,
carving initials into the forest,
totems to carriaged love.

We were queens moving cosmos,
shepherds with wineskins,
geniuses full of untapped DaVincis,
parcels too precious to drop.

Don't you hear the trumpet songs
and nearby interpreters explaining

the hieroglyphic figures?
It's a never-ending riddle:
the siren song with its lute and lyre,
the rhythm of the saints
parading past the temple steps,
rekindling medieval songs and Shakespearean flax.
In one hand the Talmud, in the other Dostoevsky.

This is no meager potion,
we've moved beyond the spells.
This is writing on an abandoned sky.
Deny me not my pen, my rite of passage.

At the Ranch

In those days, I lived in an antique barn.
The roof over my head was made of tin,
and the walls were collaged with pin-up women.
I sat in my bathrobe with men twice my age,
and we talked of cinemascope wonders.

"Women rule it all," they told me.
"Women decide the world."

I was free.
With a year abroad in my peddling can,
I wrapped by hair up on top of my head,
just like my mother used to do.
In the toolshed, I sanded down wood
to make mirrors and mantles and mischief.

There were headdresses to wear and
photo shoots to be taken and
hearts to be rubbed in cloths until
they start beating again.

We were renegades.
Off the grid, Marlon Brando and Audrey Hepburn
were our friends and at night, in the avocado groves,
I could smell the cherimoyas.

It was a temporary situation.

Soon, I packed my suitcases
for the blue and white house nearby.
The first things we moved in were his
hunting rifle and a vacuum.
It was all very standard —
he would hunt the venison and
I'd provide a reason for a shower curtain.
He would bring me tea.
I'd write the list of what we needed for love
and tack it to the refrigerator.

These days, it was foreign films and Westerns.
My father didn't call much then.

Around me grew twin dogs and men,
a farmer and an artist.
We ate badly burnt French toast with
overgrown berries and sketched
our future novels.
When life threw molasses,
we walked into the mountains and
carved sticks beside the river.
There was no talk of money or clothes.
We had neither and both.
Slowly the avocados grew into buds.

We lived in a valley.
Before that, we lived on a hill
where the horses woke each day,

flaring nostrils and grain.
It was my unknown sendoff.

Before men were the women,
walking hills saying prayers to the moon,
grasping hands and dancing in twilight.
Sunlight had nothing on our eyes.
We were gold dust, flecks of strength,
diamonds, rolling through the hillsides,
queens of the dirt on our shoes.
At night we swirled,
Sufi dancers awaiting the good story,
dreaming of gardens and film scripts,
while calico lamps illuminated the mantle
and brass statues hung on our wall.
In those days, we never used the oven.

It was the haven of goddesses.

Cherry Blossoms

It takes 351 days to arrive.
Each March peering out the winterscape
counting down the sunrises until
the last puff of clouds rise
over the Kumano Kodo,
the Kii mountains fading in the distance
as the final pilgrims
make their way to their floor,
roll flat their shiki mats,
line their shoes side by side,
and wash the day off their hands —
fingers rubbing back and forth
under water poured from bamboo
ladles that rest beside the
limestone dragon's mouth.

And then, they wait.

I hear patience is part of the purification,
silence the requiem of the symphony.
The birds sing quietly from barren branches,
the woods quite shy 'til spring.
Three seasons and a morning sparrow,
a single bud begins.

What we have paused for has come.
Fifty weeks of tedious landscape

for ten tiny days of bloom.

These hours: so precious.
This life: so fragile.

Hapax

We rose early
in the land of the coca leaves,
our hair pinned down like bonnets
beneath the mosquito nets
in which we slept,
brown weathered hands awaking us
to the smell of toasted arepas
smoldering in browned oil,
open fire smoke flickering past
the horses' nostrils, who carried
medicine and the world on their backs.

It had been four sleeps in this jungle,
our guides in recovery as much as
the rest of us, nineteen experts
on the way to the Ciudad Perdida,
a crew of doctors, lawyers, poets,
led by former forced militia, runners of
a drug trade perpetuated by
northern neighbors in need of
inflated awakeness.

Here, we slept in peace.

La Ciudad Perdida
city no longer lost,
we sat in your Colombian dust

around a circular fire at eve —
it seemed the proper way —
each day beginning and ending *en fuego*,
recovering the flecks in our eyes
long buried like the ruins on which
we hovered.

What horrors make a city abandon itself?
What successes make us vacate our souls?

These were not the questions we were churning
as we sat next to the Mamo priest,
white beard bending down toward his
fingers, carving wooden pipes,
whittling the survival of the ages.
For three thousand years while the world forgot,
five families remained for open-eyed
star gazing, fresh-ground herbs, and octogenarian
lifespans, while we chose hand held screens and
pharmaceuticals.

This wasn't a comparison of civil and primitive.
Our Socratic method was less than complete,
the passerby tourists and the ancient priests
breaking leaves at fireside, each positing
evidences for wholeness in their
various tongues.

Twenty-one villagers left in the mud huts,

burning sage, barefoot children playing soccer
with tin cans, tiny feet walking
two days into town for school,
giant minds mastering every speck of
mountain range, pointing the way
back to progress.

I sat in between the doctor and priest,
each in the midst of their own dissertation,
two divergent liturgies blending
survival and extinction.
The Mamo priest spoke in Kogi:
guardian of mother creation,
jaguar protector of the hearts of
shrubs, species, and skin.
The doctor, in his studied vein,
meanwhile found solace in Greek:
the theory of *hapax*,
the extinguishing breath,
words that appear but once in a tale
and then are forever lost.

If souls are words,
and existence a poem,
our deaths cause
a whole world to perish.
The hapax has spoken.
The jaguars roam.
The fire is permanently extinguished.

Here in the rubble, the tomb raiders are obvious,
the dust still wedged on our shoes.
Elbow to shoulder,
we sift through bronzed idols,
wondering who will excavate
our future resurrections.

Before They Hired Judy

I memorized the mantra,
clicked red heels three times fast,
but all I saw was you:
like a circus tribe,
fearful and insatiably ignorant.

By now, I was far from home.

I cursed the ground for the magic ball,
the festering broom,
all the things we deemed as evil.
These pagan shrouds, those crystal spheres,
that could make You disappear.

I cut the scene, turned off the tape,
and stared You in the eye,
demanding back my life,
but my words bounced off your chest,
like bullets hitting tin.
I will not let you keep me here.
Give me back my pulse.
But the director came back on the set
and told me to be nice
and told me to look pretty
and told me to play numb (like You).
And the lights came on
and the fog turned pink

and they floated a bubble on set with a string
for a god they claimed was good.

So I burned her house,
and I lost my job.
And I've seen too much,
but I've found my faith.
And I tried to block off all the roads
that had me slumbering in poppies.

But the beating heart's the last to go,
so don't dare you call it wicked.

Golden Fleece

I heard the sirens singing off the coast of Crete.
It was an illusion I'll believe in fully.
I tied myself upon the mast and moistened the words
again in my mouth that would satiate this need.
You are not alone. It is not your fault.
I stroked an oar into the sand
and the tide washed a thousand marks away,
confirming all suspicions.

The world will tempt you to be small, clench tight
your fist and preview all your wisdom.
Ignore the memo.
They were not the first to type it out
in fear and you are not the first to burn
it back in love.
Make haste to banish lies.
Turn the rudder from the island
mirage and set your face like flint
into the wind.

From there, begin to row.
Faster, tighter, 'til your breath pours
down your brow in droplets of dew-like
sweat and while the others scream the
world is flat, keep pushing towards the edge.
I will meet you there.
There we will be free.

The Flip Side of Oz

I keep thinking about what you had to say
a few songs back
about freedom
and the way morning
breaks you open and the possibilities
that brokenness allows.

I keep thinking about what she had to say
about direction and homelands,
and the way we notice everything except
what is most essential and everyone except
who is really by our sides.

Thousands of steps I've waltzed in these
shoes, awaiting the angels to flutter,
watching the brick melt beneath my feet
with few signs of progress.
I've carried my map full
of fairies and wishes, surrounding
my senses with fools, demigods, lions,
and everything else that haunts me.

There's no magic wand
that sets this world at ease.
There's only hope. Exquisite hope.
Behind the curtain, a flash of lights.
Afar no longer scares me.

EDEN

Let us sing the brightness of hours
and holiness of rivers.
The delight of burnt sienna
and the foolishness of dusk.
Every second, a spasm,
a praise for lemon trees laden
with wild bees.
A burning in our throats
when clouds are dressed in lace and
dirt begins to preach,
These are my brethren.
This city with no name,
we pan for gold
and bow our heads at
translucent brightness.
We've barely read the intro;
we gulp down every word.

This is the form of doves.

Three births

When you were born, hemlock trees
scattered leaves upon the soil.
Your mother watched you breathe
and marveled at your liberation.
The bright blue eyes and curly hair
of the inevitable astronaut,
scientist, and backyard tennis star.

There is no circumstance that could
stop your imagination.

When I was born, my mother
sang me lullabies on verdant hills.
She walked me through the river full
of mossy banks until I began
to see the colors.

When we were born, the forest parted,
separating oaks from pines.
I found you amidst the horses,
the wheat now grown shoulder high,
pageantry of commonplace miracles.

Move-in Day

It came silently as most things do,
except there was no camel or straw
or donkey or twilight.
It came without pomp or fog lamps or
party bag decorations.
Still, it came.

I am not here to compare my intertwining
of hands with the birth of a god,
but I wonder what happens when
huge things start silently;
does celebration exist beyond sound or is
stillness the echo through which
we overhear the angels?

And in this hush
who clocks the hours which brought us here?
The countless palpitations of hearts
and opening of sinews,
trading my mess for yours and yours for mine,
each shined cupboard spoon
reflecting back our choices.

We moved boxes that day,
sorting the past from present —
cd cases alongside lace dresses,
modern lamps and holders of antiquity.

Suitcases disappeared.

I poured through boxes of yearbooks and undershirts,
making drawers for his and hers.
And each time I return from the yard,
I still find you in my bed.

Between Lucy and Marilyn

The night before a boy became my bedmate,
I slept under makeshift covers at my
adopted mother's flat.

We drank mint soda on her sofa
and watched a documentary on Marilyn,
recovered foster child in the arms of JFK.

I dreamt and awoke to more reruns.

When you watch *I Love Lucy*,
let her teach you how to manage men,
how to get the couch you want when the boss says *no*,
while smoking in your New York apartment.

Has it always been the same story?
She needed a perm by Friday
in order to marry off her single friend by Wednesday,
and she needed a girlfriend to tell Ricky
why she couldn't stand his couch.
She baked lasagna in heels
while mocking the ego of Cuba,
smiling and shining his shoes.

Meanwhile, Marilyn swirled in her dress,
lipstick that changed America.

So tell me, girls,
I'm now organizing linens
and he's sorting through the bills.
Shall we label them *his* and *hers?*

Hatching

Last June I saw a chick hatch herself,
pecking every fleck of shell until she could exhale.
Instincts enough to break beyond the barriers
and when she did, she crumpled,
panting on fresh earth.

From across the warmed glass, I whispered,
It takes a lot to arrive.
She collapsed down in the hay and
slept 'til daybreak when the gulls flew overhead
to guide her first steps.

And what are we here to do but bear witness?
And who is seeing all this striving
to tell her she's alive?

But maybe that's how the geese get home,
their departure long before winter's crest,
each wing pointed toward an unknown town.

Bloodlines

I found your grandfather
from two generations back
laying on the roadside,
napping beneath doorknobs and doorbells,
and he held me like a child.

Do you not remember how efficient it is
to look for signs and signals,
ancestors pushing hearts together
from empty house to grain filled barn.

Love is a matter of momentum.
My sky at your back,
your fingertips on my eyelids.
We've been covered in white snow
for ages, awaiting the fire
of time to melt narrow tunnels,
sledding me to your side.

I find you at bedtime, at morning time,
at the ancient time, wearing cuff links
and straw hats,
barefoot, awake.
We are random faces facing each other
as brother and sister,
lover and friend.
This strange countenance

pressing me with questions,
the chivalry of daisies.

Relics

We spent our days being guided by priests and saints,
village women and antique books,
pages unread so long —
there was little aberration to the plot.

You picked me sarsaparillas,
while I read you Hildegard.
We folded postcards on the Rhine
and bathed in the river our ancestors traversed.

Each day we could not keep as before.

When we pulled up to Wuppenhau,
I admit I was doubtful —
nothing there but borrowed tools,
a diner full of factory men,
and a locked steeple door.

After searching the cemetery
for stones and names we could not remember,
we met a man with dissolved hair
and wire-rimmed glasses
who told us the story we sought
was no longer there.

He asked us to follow him.

Three towns over,
we learned that it was possible.

We traced our fingers on the edge
of a journal, touching the ink
that our forefathers used to
record their union tale.
It wasn't long before the man
placed holy water on our brows
and led us into the abbey
where the world lay frozen for
500 years and Columbus' globe
still spun next to leather-bound
parchments and Hippocrates medicine
healed us like alchemy,
transmuting past to present
between two beautiful forevers.

On Certainty

Belief comes after
the mind exhales,
the moment you lay breathless on the dirt
and say *yes.*

Belief comes after
the proof is no longer a prize,
when art will not reduce to algorithms
and honorable mentions are no longer needed
for love.

Remember how a naked child learns to see —
they clutch you in between their
mouth and fingers and feel you whole.

There are fields of questions beyond this ravine,
but I want to know what songs make you alive,
the way dawn bursts out laughing,
the way a baby gazes into light.

Opal

If white had a smell, it would be apple grass from
Virginia mountainsides at morning,
and then it would be mowed.

If white had a tint, it would glow like vapor
off the fire's peak, the early alps of winter frost,
or starlight uninterrupted.

If white had a form, it would be far from
hospital walls or picket fences
or flagrant attempts at righteousness.

Innocence is an infectious paradise.

Closed Doors

I owe my life to those I didn't love
and who could never love me back.
For the sake of the children
who never arrived,
I thank you.
The summer geraniums you never brought me,
and the lyrics I never wrote you.
There is no reason not to drink to
the men, the ladies,
all who have called out for love
and never knew why they held
open their raw and empty hands.
These are the proofs beyond progress.
The bloodline that never formed,
the most persuasive thesis
giving birth to unthinkable kin.

Percolate

Would that you were here instead of not,
the fuel I'd crave would change. And you:
I'd brew a cup, slip down well and slow the shot,
my drink, a quench for thirst, first hot then cool.

No sugar please — I'd take you black, ground beans
from earth rinsed once. The grounds I'd press
with steam 'til drip by drip the water leans
into my mug.

Once used for herbs, now nothing less
than coffee fills and fuels my swig. I'd sip
down drip by drip, brown dirt now raised to tonic
thick, from mire to mirth, from cup to lip,
aroma sweet, I'd breathe away the logic.

And Adam danced with God, the gardens still.
Mere water not enough.

Processions

This is the moment that turns us inside out,
do not pass go until I've bought you your haven
and brought you home —
an opened-armed welcome
which spins us around in the nick of time,
as the band begins to tune
and the entry slows down the music.
A full change of scene where roses grow beyond dirt
and heels dig into earth
to grow a man out of a boy and a woman out of
girlhood.

I'll cue you in, he says.
You scoff because he hasn't cued anything
yet in his life,
the stumbler upon the good,
always the apprentice.
But you hear his beat,
which matches his pulse, and it thumps
and it bleeds and maybe, just maybe,
the one you've been waiting for your whole life
sees you under his own skin,
two becoming one,
veil lifting from your brow,
hands descending down your nape,
to breathe you in,
gut to soul,

to let you in,
presence beyond doubt,
fingers grasping for truth that screams,
This is what I want.

And you fight for it,
clasp hands for it,
trade hearts for it,
for the whole world is watching
this candlelit stage that you've crafted for love.

But the flame won't singe —
the sparks burning out the ages,
smoking all the seconds of waste and pain.
All the broken cardiacs and bloody knuckles
climbing toward this moment where

two become one,
eyes locked tight,
nodding in unison,
banging souls into cymbals until
the beat turns on,
from *I to Thou,*
where fear turns to love and
love turns to fuel and the wick
grows bright as a torch
as the saints come marching in.

Vows

With this ring, I thee vow
to do impossible things
on an inescapable earth
and under various names
repeating prayers from the ancients,
I sketch my hopes in the sand
and declare you my home.

What strengthens me will uphold you
and what joys you will fasten me
and when you have nothing left
save playing cards and bingo chips,
I will hold you by my side convinced
you are my morning miracle.

The saints say it's somehow possible
to commit each day to patient hope.
Forgive me, dear,
I am no saint,
but this I vow thee here —
this hundred years
a lightning bolt
of daily bread and wine —
we shall spread the feast together
in open joy and ceaseless praise,
noting every simple abundance
and grateful for every daybreak.

Whatever I hold in my hand:
a parchment, a prayer, a success, a child
is yours for the holding
and beholding.

Whatever I dream in my dreams:
a future, a homestead, a canopy of daisies
is yours for the sharing
and feast.

Today I wear my Sunday best
and tomorrow, be my forever best
as life do us join
and death do us part.

And should thieves come near
to steal our hope,
fret not:
I have a quiver full and vision straight,
and with my tiny arrow
I will aim for stars and
drag a narrow ray of sunlight
to your side,
our lights a circle wider than any shadow.

GRACES & GRATITUDES

To my mother, who gifted me words.
To my friends, who fill life with story.
To my husband, who inspires my mornings.
To my professors, who've crafted my lines.
To Liz, who edits my commas.
To my Godmother, who gifts me thick books.
To love, which keeps us all writing letters home.

About the Book

We all search for homes,
the garden from which we stem
and inexplicably long to return.
This imprint of innocence cannot be torn from us,
no less than our childhood imaginations
can be locked in treasure chests
and buried in our pasts.
We all have eaten great feasts
east of Eden, drizzling in paradises
of love, God, warm dirt,
planting gardens in havens of others,
marriages, and hands which hold us.
With honey still on our lips,
we too are survivors of exile,
carriers of doubts, riddles, and
fictions which claim we are alone.
This world is wild.
We live in a technicolor Oz,
our reality but a shadow.
Together, we tape the globe together with
strings, illusionary boundaries of countries,
colors and skin.
Home: our constant search.
Home: our constant companion.
We travel far to find ourselves
and sing our urgent hallelujahs.

Jennifer Strube is an educator, artist,
therapist, and dark chocolate fiend.
When she was a little girl,
she was obsessed with Dorothy.
At age 12, she started writing tragic love poems,
while playing MASH and Girl Talk board games.
By college, she spent summers abroad
and wistfully wrote home love letters.
While finishing grad school in Asia,
she filled her nights with eighties cover bands
and streets that felt familiar.
Six months later, she returned home.
Six months later, he arrived.
This work debuted at her wedding in New Orleans,
when she read her husband her *Vows* and
placed gold in his palm.
Together, they share a tree house with their cat, Ro.
Follow more of her musings at:

www.jenniferstrube.com
Instagram: @jenniferstrube
Facebook: @jenniferlstrube
Twitter: @jenniferstrube7